SCENES
FROM THE
LIVE POETS'
SOCIETY

SCENES
FROM THE
LIVE POETS'
SOCIETY

◆

**A Selection of Poems
by members of the
Live Poets' Society
of Santa Fe,
New Mexico**

◆

FIRST EDITION 2001

10 9 8 7 6 5 4 3 2 1

LIBRARY OF CONGRESS CATALOG CARD NUMBER: 2001 135812
ISBN: 0-9711831-0-4 paper

PUBLISHED BY:
THE LIVE POETS' SOCIETY
433 Paseo de Peralta, Suite 101
Santa Fe, New Mexico 87501

The Live Poets' Society wishes to thank Caroline Ravenfox, John Bishop, Jayn Stewart, Victor di Suvero, and Sabrina Coryell for compiling and editing this book.

PREFACE

They arrive in jeans... their shirts and blouses are multi-colored... they join the
conversation circle. Is it the 60's... a love-in... or a later generation... a holistic
healing session? No, none of these... or a touch of each?
   It's a quarterly meeting of the Live Poets' Society!

The Live Poets' Society (LPS) consists of artists, business persons, consultants, political activists, engineers, lawyers, philanthropists, educators and more. We range in age from the early thirties to the mid-seventies; approximately 50/50 male and female. Combined, we have lived at one time or another in many parts of the world and have survived wars, pestilence, and other forms of social upheaval.

Somehow each of us separately discovered the magic in the mountains of northern New Mexico. It is here that we have found the courage to share what had been for many of us a lifelong secret: we each write poetry.

I was fortunate enough to find a number of poets among my friends. Friends whose lives on the surface did not really reflect their poetic abilities and sensibilities. I first identified and then captured each one of these friends in vulnerable moments—those moments when we would admit to the singular clandestine activity of writing poetry.

"...but what do you do for yourself, your guts? How do you feed your soul?" was my approach to a potential "live poet." Each of us responded with hesitance and relief. Thus, LPS was born.

Within two years we had grown to twenty people (now more than thirty), meeting every two to three months to share our secret passion. Rumors about our curious gatherings took hold in the Santa Fe community and we were asked to perform publicly on radio. That was our first step "out of the closet." Later we were invited to perform "live" at a local coffeehouse/bookstore, another aMUSEing step. We were sensational!

Strong friendships have emerged within the group, as well as strong loyalties. In a sense, we are a support group, an intellectual group, an emotional group, and a sounding board for ideas and feelings.

We are a mystical, strange, and probably weird bunch, delighted by our participation in life and in LPS. Perhaps we are like you; perhaps our musings will encourage more "closet poets" to seek out one another. We hope so.

RICHARD BRANDT
Founder

Present Members of the Live Poets' Society

Saul Balagura, John Bishop, Richard Brandt, Sandor Brent, Victor di Suvero, Jessica Elkins, Doris Fields, Henry Finney, Lisa Fisher, Beverly Fox, Anna Gallegos y Reinhart, Marcia Gell-Mann, Gary Max Glazner, Trudy Healy, Honorable Wyatt Heard, Gerry Hotchkiss, Linda Jamison, Bonnie Lupien, Marge McLauchlin, Caroline Ravenfox, Robert Rhodes, Charley (Cheryl) Romney-Brown, John Rubel, Michael Sutin, Dodie Thomas, Arden Tice, and Pamela Wolff

Distant Out-of-Town Members

Jerry Cajko, Patricia Casey, Sabrina Coryell. Brother John Fairfax, Halsted, Katie Peters, and Sally Ann Rosenberg.

Poets Contributing
to this volume

Saul Balagura

SAUL BALAGURA was born in Cali, Colombia, in 1943 almost a decade after his parents emigrated from Romania. He showed an early interest in painting that culminated with his first solo exhibition at the age of seventeen. After obtaining his medical degree he went into self-exile, emigrating to the United States. After receiving a doctorate degree in Biopsychology from Princeton University, he taught first at the University of Chicago and later at the University of Massachusetts. During these years he conducted basic science research projects that resulted in sixty scientific publications. In 1974 he re-entered the medical field and studied to become a neurosurgeon, graduating in 1980 from Albert Einstein/Montefiore Medical Center in New York, and practicing as a neuro-surgeon for fifteen years. During this time he published many clinical studies, including several on original surgical techniques. In 1994, following a strong desire to dedicate himself fully to the arts, he retired from his practice of neurosurgery and opened a studio in Tesuque, New Mexico. From this studio he has pursued in earnest the loves of his life, painting and writing. His artistic output has been exhibited in various galleries and museums throughout the United States.

CHRISTMAS JOY

It was a beautiful
fire,
as far as fires go,
that lit the old house
that once Muslim was.
It was a cold and damp
day in winter
on that particular morning
when the warmth
of the flames embraced
the yellowing pictures that hung
like melting memories
from those walls
of centuries old,
embedded with the essence
of garlic and onion
and cabbage and lamb;
and the smell of children
playing and crying
and the toothless face
of wrinkled grandma and
the missing finger in father's hand.
It was also cold and clammy
when the Pope spoke
from his Vatican window
to the Christian crowds below
and how they rejoiced!
It was the very instant
when the Christian Serbs left
the ransacked house burning
on that Christmas day.

(1995)

FEELING

I walk into the darkness
of my Tesuque night
sensing a God so close,
perhaps hidden
behind a million stars
that gaze above me
like a million tears—of angels—
of happiness.
Perhaps he hides
behind the Pinon trees
that whistle softly
when the wind caresses
their hardened leaves
that a hundred
rainless days and nights
have not wilted.
Or he may be
inside the massive boulders
that like giant sentinels
stand over a land
so warm and delicate
that holds the imprints
of chirping little birds
during the making of love.
But I feel God so close to me
in these moonless nights,
that he could be hiding behind
a pebble close to my feet,
and that is why
I walk with such reverence
that I feel my own tears rushing like a mountain stream.

(1994)

LATE SUMMER SWIM
(Babi-Yar memories)

Come,
come with me,
come,
let us go
under this summer day,
and bathe
on the lake
at Babi Yar.
Do you hear?
Do you hear
the excitement,
the children shouting,
the parents' concerns?
They all will bathe
by the lake
in this summer day.
Dip,
dip your foot
on the warm waters,
soft as velvet,
by the edge of Babi Lake,
and shed
your clothing
over green grasses.
Take a deep breath,
fill your lungs
with the smell
of fresh dug earth
and the excitement
of gun powder
and the gelatinous
clinging blood,
and jump with all the others
into Babi Yar Lake.

WIDE-EYED SOFT SPOKEN BEING

I sometimes awaken
in the depth of night
to find myself
under the noon's sky
and wonder out
of the comer of an eye:
Why ?

Why I who have all almost,
see the shadow
projected on the ground
by a multicolored plumed bird
and
Why do I see the fallen tree
amidst the standing forest
of living greens
even though I never
hungered for a piece of bread,
and
Why when all laugh
my mouth just wrinkles
in a smile
and
Why in a magnificent dusk
when the mountains in the distance
crown themselves in
warm magentas
do I feel forgotten, Why ?

At the distance in time
eighty years before today
and thousands of miles away
in a place called Atlanta
in our planet Earth,
a man was lynched
by a crowd of men,

(continued)

and their wives
waited at home
feeding their children hate,
and the Law never
punished then or now those men
that hung an innocent man.

And the shadow projected
by the dangling, thin,
wide-eyed soft spoken being
that once responded
to the name of Leo,
Leo Frank,
blackens my universe,
makes me hunger,
makes me thirst,
makes me see the darkness
makes me pain,
makes the days grow shorter
and the nights infinitely long
when Leo Frank just dangles
and the men who hung him run.

(1995)

DECAY

Covered by thorns
my skin is weeping
like the Gods'
when man ran away
floating in winds
of despair
hitting like a badly placed
weather vane
against a window seal.
Waving arms
like windmill's fingers
to the storm
one group of bigots
stabbing another
with the smiling face
of beatitude.
Mankind destroying mankind
under the banner of love,
putrid temples of false stars
pacing back and forth
on a stage begging for gold
as the flock crawls
in the poverty of their homes,
while politicians plunder
the spirit of nations
with no punishment
for their crimes
while all along they cry with us
from their fortress

(continued)

of hypocrisy
watching passively
their people die
as corollaries of their thoughts.
And then we ask for God
when we who know better know
that after seeing
what his creation had done
he threw himself
into the blackest black hole
in the most remote galaxy
he had made
when he thought it would
have been nice to create a world.

(1998)

John Bishop

John Bishop—I love music in the morning. I love to dance in sacred session. I am in intimacy with other beautiful Beings. I grew up in Sedona in the fifties in Northern Arizona and have lived in Santa Fe for the past fifteen years. I enjoy exploring the outer realms of physics and nanotechnology and manifesting possibilities in business. I enjoy writing poetry, playing guitar and writing songs. I enjoy making love. I travel in dimensions of Light and Love. I enjoy being. Blessings to You.

We used to play
Up on Indian Hill
Arrowheads, pottery and shards
Even found a grave one time
Little man
Curled up
In a ball
With bone beads
Strung around his neck.
We'd talk around the affairs
Of the world
Racing
Sports
Jannie Mae
And Mary Lou
As we hiked up Camelrock
And played
Down by the creek.
Apples and orchards
Peaches and pie
We grew up here Sedona
Rodeos Red rocks
Schnebly Hill
And the Slides.
Well there's a bunch of houses
Built on Indian Hill
And they call Grasshopper Flats
The West Side
But we all realized
There was something
About growing up here
That gave us roots
When we had our
First grade reunion
And I found out
I still love
Jannie Mae.

(continued)

She's got those eyes
And puffy lips that
Draw you into
Her Santiago smile
Baby of six
Mother of one
Men alluring around her.

"That is why," her brother said,
"That is why."
"She's da baby of the family
You know."

She's with Mateo now
Great Italian chef
Makes home made pizza
Kiss the fingers good
Twenty four, like Leonardo
Beautiful and sweet
They get in a fight
He almost leaves to go back to Maui
Where they lived on their plot
Near a tropical forest
With no electricity
In an unfinished house
Made love by the moon
Rode with the sun.

Andreas has come
Father of the child
Passionate lover
Ex-husband
"We still are one
How could you be with him
These other men
I am jealous and dangerous
You vagabond whore
You are mine
(continued)

I desire you
Where you be
I will be there
To parent our child
Dream of our romance
Dance with our passion."

I was wondering what you'd be like
I dreamed of you
Where I smelled your body
Watched you dress
Every strand of hair
Laying on your shoulders
Rosa, I know you feel me looking.

There's a rose by the river
A fresh bud grows
Early morning shower
Welcomes the new dawn.

Born with passion
Nectar of the night
Flowing emotion
Room of delight.

Take me down to the river
Take me down to the room
Making love in the morning
Full rose in bloom.

Into the depths
Of our kiva we dance
Snake in our mouth
Rain from our eyes.

I bow my head
And walk a path
Worn by time
In sandstone cliffs
By ancient Anasazi.

Great spirit
Inner core
Butterfly
Corn.
Take me
To a place
Of serenity
And knowing.

Man
Woman
Did they understand?
Was love
As complicated then?

Into the depths
Of our kiva we dance
Snake in our mouth
Rain from our eyes.

As dew drops glisten
Purple iris flowers
Sing to my
New mistress
In the morning
I'll be there
To hold you
And caress you.

Rising from the tide
The fog rolls in
It's a day for you
And for me
To cuddle
And feel the song
Of our hearts
Blend in perfect harmony.

Can this be
Can this really be?
All my life
I've been wrapped
In a shroud
Of what should be.

And here I am
In love with you
As I wake from my dream
And wonder
What might have been.

Translucent stone
Rocks on fire
Floor of sage
Branch and hide.

Pass the pipe
Herbs and sweet grass
Twelve hours hot
Sweat and prayer.

Water. Water.
So very hot.
Face to the floor
Lungs on fire.

Journey to the spirit world
Where we all must dwell
Initiation
Purification
Sweat lodge
Ho.

This journey we take into the unknown
We navigate our ship, while we be here,
On solid ground, on solid ground.

Yes, it is simple when we turn to the Light.
We turn to the Light
Leave our beliefs behind. Our beliefs behind,
Our overlays, imprints, Mom and Dad
All those overlays, we relax now that web
And be Pure Essence looking out.
There we be. Divine Presence in human form.

We turn to the Light
Leave our beliefs behind.
We turn to the Light
And know the beloved inside.
Beloved Being.
There we be in intimacy.
And there we be with others
All Beloved Beings.

I be there with You now
We be strong. In joy. In love. In relation.
We be here now ships sailing
On the ocean of life. Ships in relation.
Relationships in complete freedom to sail.
I sail with you now my Beloved.

We sail in complete freedom
To be the Light. I say to You,
You have compete freedom
To be the Light. Always.
To be that gift for yourself
To be that gift for all your relations
You have complete freedom.

This journey we take into the unknown
We navigate our ship, while we be here
On solid ground, on solid ground.

Richard Brandt

RICHARD BRANDT

BIOGRAPHY
requires
GEOGRAPHY

And in this case—
LEXICOGRAPHY

Born: YES
Location at Birth: PLANET EARTH
Location Now: PLANET EARTH

Having spent most of my life
between mathematics and the entertainment industry,
why did I invent the Live Poets' Society?

Answer: (PLEASE FILL IN)

CANYON CONFLUENCE

where water, land . . . and perhaps some people . . . find each other

Have I tasted too quickly of the sacred Datura
      and dreamed the lazy, easy canyons floating by
On both sides, wedged by Earth's own artistry
      interrupted here and there by Anasazi yearnings —
Who decides the colors of the land,
      the rusts, the greys, the turquoise, the beige
          against the azure
              and the cotton-ball clouds

Have I thirsted too much for the sacred Datura
      reviving dim glimpses of Folsom wanderings and work
Why call the river mud-laden
      that mundane imagery fails to translate truth —
Not mud, but rich sedimentary sweepings
      a wondrous mineral treasure-house
          in which I float
              and cool my soul

Have I trusted too easily the sacred Datura
      to grant me walloping flashes of wild white water,
Of rocks and rapids, rushing and tumbling
      throughout a roaring reckless fearful fantasy —
Infamous "Big Drop," its great limestone forms and shapes,
      its ancient lands, worn down,
          worn away, careening
              liquid highway

No, I fed not upon the sacred Datura
Rather inhaled the fragrance of her trumpets
      for she is merely the lowly jimsonweed —
      and I, much smaller than the canyon bluffs

                    1987

Written while rafting on the Green and Colorado Rivers. Datura (common name: Jimsonweed) has trumpet-shaped blossoms and is known to be highly hallucinatory.

SPIRITUS INTERRUPTUS

ours

was a non-stop rapid-fire conversation that never ended
obliterated time and extended
constantly pleasing and ceaselessly flowing
relentlessly growing regardless of distance
or outside resistance until

one day you said,

"Stop!"

and hung up the phone like turning the corner
from Bright-Broadway into
a black
cul-de-sac.

ours

was a playful confiding in whispers eliding sweet sibilant
rounds of incredible sounds with residual brilliance
and verbal resilience transmitting our thoughts
and receiving retorts while entreating replies
of quite meaningful size when

abruptly you screamed,

"Halt!"

and slammed the door sharply on all of my visions
of future contentment and left a resentment that
drips from my faucet
and shatters my quiet
and rumples my bed-sheets.

1976

WORD PERFECT

It is strange to seal letters with wax
And impress your own mark on their backs
One senses the sprinkled perfume
The soft etch of a finely formed plume

Now the magic is no longer there
Words zip thru the atmosphere
By computer, E-mail and fax
And "vobiscum" arrives before "pax"

Sometimes the slower pace
   lets us
     step
     away
       and see the race

Those were days when ladies well-graced
Wore ribbed satin with waists tightly laced
During minuets erotic hints flirt
From tell-tale whispers of a taffeta skirt

Thus I'll honor my wondrous nostalgia
The romance of remembered regalia
I shall still send a letter or two
Writ by hand for my lover to view

1995

MY GOOD FRIEND
(Third Person Singular)

"I am your friend," she said
  Her hand made circles as she talked
        She told me briefly of my recent death
        And of my wasted life and final breath
  I never believed her.

"I am your friend," she said
  With chilled chablis and ice in her glass
        "That young man Michael's only seventeen—
        He still can be what Richard might have been"
  I stared into her eyes.

        Firelight blessed one-half her face
        And caught her cat-like subtle grace
        In cafe darkness, she explained to me
        Richard's fight with immortality.
        She talked of brilliance, art and talents
        Betrayed in Richard's search for balance.
        The iron-bound and unrelenting
        Integrity that kept preventing
        Reality from touching chance
        And all the webs of circumstance.

        She told of novels uncomposed
        Of lyric songs left undisclosed
        Of courage laced with mini-meaning
        And rooms that didn't need such cleaning.

"I am your friend," she said
  She leaned forward so I'd catch her whisper
        And told me of her love, her deep affection
        How Richard could have made their lives perfection
  I thought I listened well.

(continued)

"Are you my friend?" I said
 My face not even inches from her touch
        "Can you not feel freedom's driving rain
        A-cleansing out the clouds from Richard's brain?"
 A tear spilled on her cheek.

        In turtleneck and jeans, I answered back
        Supplying faith to fill in Richard's lack
        Describing break-outs from his old routine
        Now praising passion, not the golden mean.
        With stein in hand, proclaiming my intention
        To clarify his struggle with convention
        And unveil how near to death he truly came
        While relinquishing his mortal grasp on fame.

        I spoke of how his friends no longer greet him
        His adversaries lost their need to beat him
        His transcendental soul reveals resplendence
        Contented in its quest for independence.

"You are my friend," I said
 My fingers felt the brightness of her hair
        "For Richard's sake, for Richard's goal, I'm here
        And still my insides screech with anxious fear."
 She shifted in her chair.

"We are good friends," we said
 And nodded to some faces near the bar
        We talked of outer space and future peace
        Agreed that pain for mankind would not cease
 And Richard disappeared.

                              SAN FRANCISCO
                              BRATSKELLAR
                              SPRING 1973

OLD MAN LEARNS — TEACHES YOUTH

Youth says
    "Touch fingers...."
Old Man replies
    "My insides quake, I cannot reach that far"

Youth says
    "Sing out...."
Old Man replies
    "My voice is dull, I cannot clear the mist"

Youth says
    "Walk bravely...."
Old Man replies
    "My blood is thick, I cannot raise my arm"

Youth says
    "There's good...."
Old Man replies
    "My mind resists, I cannot make the choice"

Youth says
    "Forever...."
Old Man replies
    "My soul defers, I cannot feel my flesh"

Old Man silently considers

    Sometimes the pains in my stomach decline
    Often after a tumbler of white jug wine
        Yet only for a brief and tempting moment

    In airplanes, on long flights, there is relief
    Isolation comforts my self-inflicted grief
        Yet only for a brief and tempting moment

    Shutting out worlds, a welcome sleep grants calm
    Nature's ancient cure-dispensing balm
        Yet only for a brief and tempting moment

(continued)

Old Man silently wonders

Is there a clear signal that the end is near
Does that fearful Angel of Death give us warning
Will I recognize the subtle code
That informs me of a shortened future

Is it just a doctor sharing knowledge
That an overpowering force will soon befall
Or a supernatural ringing in my brain cells
Before some lightning strikes me in the field

ANGEL OF DEATH explains

"Examine then how nature deals with endings
Consider the mountain aspen or the river cottonwood
....as summer fades to fall"

ANGEL OF DEATH continues

"A radiant burst of brilliance...blinding sunlit yellow
A moment of beauty unsurpassed even during blossom time
....a thrilling celebration of life"

ANGEL OF DEATH concludes

"Is not that the signal of a glorious finale
Announcing the impending snow white winter frost
....when the leaves turn brown and fall"

Youth says
    "I'm frightened...."
Old Man replies
    "My eyes light up, I see the future well"

(continued)

Youth says
    "It's darkness...."
Old Man replies
    "My heart beats loud, now listen, I will tell"

Old Man teaches

    "An apocalyptic splendor is the moment we await
    To inform us of our very near demise
    As nature sends her perfect blessed Angel
    With her overwhelming wing-spread, warm and wise

    We will sparkle like the starlight on a vivid autumn night
    Our Earthly pains and cares will outward flow
    An unforeseen epiphany, awareness
    Dear youth.... Oh! What a wondrous way to go!"
                                     1995

PLAIN TALK

I like people who grow things
They move the land with a purpose
                direct
                    uncompromising.

There's power in people who plant
        and sow
        and move the soil.
I like people who let dirt
            run through
                their
                    fingers.

Some people never grow things
        they use soil
            as a verb.
              1968

Jerry Cajko

JERRY CAJKO

Born in Passaic, New Jersey....1941

There is a lot of gypsy in me....

I am of Czech and Lithuanian
    descent....

I am a man just like any other man, unlike any other
    man....

A son...husband...father...lover....

An artist...poet...sailor....AT PEACE.

VOICES DU JOUR

What fools, how blind
To think we can deceive
For free enterprise, convey deception
Delete love for gold
Add despair, de facto, dubious means

Promotion of meaningless trash
Civilization is the chirping viewed and heard
Voices of mankind in the far horizon, lost
Voices yet heard, crying out, help me — care
Voices wrapped in humble homespun of colorless hues
Deliver those where deliverance is due
Poverty, disease our worst disgrace
Handed to our fellow humans
—Given only pain as their reward

Send a message, what can I do, I can care
Give your heart to those restricted, motionless
Those locked in Pandora's box forever
Clear their pain, give a dream to the beloved many
—Or the beloved few

Unbind your heart, bound in self and fear
To those in the bottomless pit, black
Souls toady, souls tonight
Fill their hearts with warmth, gone cold

Kiss their tears away, stay — stay
Become a hero to your soul
Pick the blossoms of your talents, now!
Give in to the voices of your heart
Hold those fingerless hands of friends
—Reach out now, tonight, du jour —

TIME IS ESSENCE

Ticking—clicking—monitored in Red

Digital blinking—no thinking

Plug it in—

Wind it up—

Set the alarm—Press the button

Tick-Tock, where is my clock!

Bigger numbers, no bells or gears

Bigger numbers, bigger fears

Tragic noises, no real tunes

Ticking, clanking, wake up soon!

I'll be late—Wait! Wait! Wait!

How can we afford time
To drift away from the realities of day
To join oneself in thought, leaving the ordinary to rest?
To find peace and quiet in the simple ways
                                        —a daydream

To relish a little of remembered times,
To pace our heart and heal in ways never tried,
To enjoy our time, unleash the mind
To listen to our heartbeat—Time...!

MARLIES

Doth my "X," my life derail

Begone my art of saintly hue

The pen becomes my sword, my veil

Begone my art? A poem blue

Doth my life at end be near

Begone my art, begin anew!

—Prepare a simple spot of ease

Where my thoughts, my body pleased

Where my lost and lingering soul

Knows no fear

Knows no tear

Knows no time

Knows no rhyme

Where the lost and lingering soul of mine

Remembers love, a love divine.

WHERE IS MY INDIA

Where is my India
Is it here, is it there
Or in apartments alone, not shared

Where is my India!
Is it here where families once one
Reside without fun or sun
In boxes, poly shades of blue
Turned gray, wrinkled, faded, unglued

Where is my India?

India is where I stay,

India may be delayed....!

from ME to THE....

pious pursuits , required salutes

rad , cool , zoned-out trite !

interviews , opinions , reality misplaced

posturing , cavorting , without grace

images of deleted fears , style out

advertising , museum & gallery blues

ART ? (HUM , $ & ¢ , $ & ¢ , $ & ¢ TRA LA)

films , fashionable clout

studio visits , professional clues

food for thought , pulp of a tree

profound bondage , according to THE

santa fe monthly , rag of the arts '93

but it's ... FREE ! ... for thee

going   going   gon#* (!)

i feel my mind going

like an ooze

through a golden grate

memory   words seem far   searching

the tongue is but a stone

behind the pearly whites . . . . . . gates ???

omm to a flower ,

the gardenia unfolds luscious petals, fragile

engulfing the senses, palpating nostrils explode

gently.....

a fragrant attraction, of creamy white

dizzy.....

swooning degrees permeate painlessly

delicate.....

delicious.....

a dervish.....

a "delirious DELILAH" dream

tropical intoxication, nirvana for the nose

octaves , la ti do.....

aroma to the sound of omm

viva , ST. LUCIA . . . .

a time on the beach
where time reflects the mountains rough

where turquoise waters cool the soles of your feet
where time stands still . . . . .

views pristine, need not be heard
water of cleansing hues, relaxes the soul and
takes me to far off thoughts

where children tasted their first salty sensations
far away waters, far away destinations,
far away names, new temptations

new worlds where children play
worlds gone astray

sunsets a millennium ago, still glow
black golden waters , laced mercury, gay
welcomes the night, then melts away . . . .

Victor di Suvero

VICTOR DI SUVERO

W ho am I? Who is this person who writes the news of this day or of a war long past and supposes that it might be of interest to a reader looking for anything at all?

I really am still trying to discover answers to these and to other questions related to the circumstances of my life and have not succeeded yet—but I am still trying.

The facts are relatively simple: Born in Turin, Italy, in 1927 the son of a Jewish father and a Catholic mother, brought up in French schools in Shanghai and Tientsin in China, emigrating with the rest of my family as a "prematurely anti-fascist" political refugee to San Francisco, California, in 1941 before the Second World War, serving as a Merchant Seaman in the Pacific during that war, graduating from U.C. Berkeley in 1949 with a B.A. in Political Science after having edited *The Occident,* the literary magazine of the University. I became a forest fire lookout and a coal-miner, a real estate and mortgage broker and a developer while writing my poetry as I went along. I married and had two children as I kept on the road. I mined sapphires in Montana and put together the world's first portable desalinating equipment on a commercial basis, established Pennywhistle Press that has been publishing poetry for more than 15 years and served on the Board of the National Poetry Association. I worked with John Lilly and his dolphins, studied Zen with Alan Watts and learned about life from Jean Varda while finding ways to meet obligations and pay bills like all the rest of us—moving to New Mexico in the late eighties where I helped to build a house, still writing, looking, learning and hoping that I might leave a flower or a poem or two that might bring a smile or a "yes!" to someone who might come along the way that I've been going.

ABOUT AGREEMENTS

Looking back, looking down the mountain side
It's all about agreements—there they are
All down in the fields, the valleys, the foothills,
All the agreements of your life, scattered—
There, there and there—those that were
Kept and those that were not—those that
Cost and those that were like presents
Discovered, sometimes by accident but more
Often by desire—also all those agreed to
Agreements that were full of reservations,
Those hold backs that made emptiness
Happen and those others made in good faith
That ended up betraying themselves.

Down there, in the litter, yes, there, also
The agreements we made with ourselves,
And then changed. The agreements we
Made with the universe, with the beloved
Of the moment, the beloved for always
More in hope than anything else

                                    and

Then all those others, the ones. where we lived
Up to the commitment and the others left
Us hanging, the ones we'd rather forget
And the ones we never will forget
Until that day comes when we check out
Whether we agree on the day and the
Hour or not it still remains a
Landscape of agreements whose colors
Are myriad and whose sense is mostly
Unknown, misunderstood, well meant
And even, in many cases, the way it
Should have been—looking back.

TO BE LOVING

To be loving is to discover reasons for life.
To be loving is to wake wonders and make
Gentleness descend with the Spring's rain.
To be loving is to forgive the past, embrace
The possible and enhance the colors of dawn.
To be loving is to enclose entire languages
In a gesture and oceans of desire in a look.
To be loving is to discover patience as a way
Of life, not as a game, nor as a trial
To be undergone without anxiety or fear.
To be loving is to recognize that the sole
Of the most beautiful foot is most beautiful
Because it supports beauty with each step
Along every road and remains true and
Constant even when it is tried by walking on fire.

To be loving one must reach into corners
One did not know existed in one's own heart
And choose to make order in the jumble usually
Found there. To be loving one must be as brave
As one can possibly be or else the battle is lost
Before it is joined and satisfaction will flee.
To be loving one must learn to hear, not
Just to listen, to distinguish, not just to see
Or count up the items presented by life.

To be loving one must learn to receive, to
Accept and to understand as well as
To give, to offer, to share and to teach.
To be loving one must come to the moment
Untrammeled by baggage, without fear
Of the consequences, with the sure knowledge
That of all the stars in the heavens
The one lighting this moment is the only
One whose light counts and is impeccable.

WHAT IS YOUR NAME?

Who are you?
Saint of the near miss, the close call?
Turning the car's wheel,
Deflecting the knife's point
So that we walk out of the hospital
The next day greeting the sun
Gratefully?

What are you, guardian angel,
Kachina, invisible spirit and friend,
You—the one who makes the judge
Hear our side of the case, who
Drops the name from the list,
Wakes the lookout on time
And makes one miss the train
That connected with the plane that goes down?

I build you this poem at dawn
Gratefully listening to the squawking of jays,
To the sound of water falling
And to the intermittent silence
Wondering how it is that so few
Know you, acknowledge you, praise you,
Saint of the near miss, the close call.

ULYSSES IN TESUQUE

Down there it was Tiresias
Who told me I would find
Peace and rest in the mountains —
If I were to go inland so far, he said
That a wayfarer I would meet
Would ask the use of the oar
I would be carrying on my shoulder.
"Would that be a winnowing flail?"
He'd ask, and then I'd set it down
And find my peace at last —
And I did that — and I did plant
My oar here and built a house —
But the grapes of my desire
Were not made into wine
And the roses in the garden
Are beaten down by summer hail
While dreams of soft sand,
Salt spume and sea shells merge
With the talk of old compañeros
Remembering Jason and the Golden Fleece —
All those things consume my nights
And eat the marrow of the years
I've left to breathe — not knowing
If the thunder roars to send me on
Back to the sea or to keep me here
Until that night that has no dawn
Comes with its mirror to find me out!

In the March 1999 issue of the Atlantic Monthly, *David M. Kennedy, Professor of History at Stanford University presented an article entitled "Victory at Sea." Professor Kennedy properly employs the historian's overview, accurately reporting data and the facts without touching on the human elements of those memorable events. The feelings and sacrifices and the personal specifics of those days are not mentioned, nor is there any mention at all of the significant supporting role played by the men and ships of the U.S. Merchant Marine, without whose involvement there would have been no Victory at all. Having sailed as an able-bodied seaman on deck on ships that performed a portion of the supply function required for all the Victories in the Pacific, from the Russell Islands to New Guinea and the Philippines, I saw and experienced aspects of those days unnoticed by Professor Kennedy. My reaction to the impersonality of his overview triggered the development of a song cycle whose view is from below, not from above, and whose intent is to flesh out the story in human terms. Here are three of the songs in the cycle, a work in progress.*

SEA SONGS

for my father, for Jim San Jule, and for all the men I sailed with in those days....

First Song
I sing of the arms of the men who carried,
Who hauled, stowed, shoved, nailed and tied
Those cargoes that made that victory at sea
Possible, that made it possible for the work
To be done before the ships even went to sea, all
Those men whose hands measured the steel
Before it was cut into the shapes that made
The hulls that would be launched to take
The places of the ones sunk in the Atlantic,
Destroyed in the Pacific and drawn ashore
On the reefs of unnamed islands from
The Aleutians to Antarctica and driven
Down into the deep by storm and gunfire.

(continued)

I sing of the arms
Of those who had honed their skills on
Steam schooners, hauling lumber from Coos Bay
And Gray's Harbor down to the mills in
Oakland, on fishing boats whose home ports
Were well hidden behind glaciers in Alaska,
On oil tankers steaming their flammable cargoes
Out of Richmond and San Pedro out to Hawaii
While their brothers on shore fought the shape up,
The longshore bosses and the ship owners.
                    I sing of those arms that were strong enough
To dance the drums of lube and other oils
Across steel decks down in the holds of-ships
And of those other arms made mostly of bone,
Of the young ones, who had more will than sense,
Who had gone down to the sea before their beards
Had grown into beards, because they wanted to help.
                    I sing for the voiceless, for all those drowned—
For all the others who found their deaths on
And above the sea's surface, were buried there
In that great silence, the great cold, until their flesh,
Their blood and their bones became once
Again part of that salt sea from which we all came.
I leave it to all those others, statisticians and
Historians, all those numerologists who write
And publish the details of battles listing
The ships that went down at Midway, the subs
That were sunk in the Atlantic with the numbers
Of those that went down with them. My interest
Does not sit in counting how this admiral
With his flagship and flag had sweated this
Battle turn or that one, and what his hunch
Had done for him, or for us, or rather to us
Out on lookout or down in the engine room
Not knowing, not ever knowing, whether
His choice, his judgment would bring us
Life or bring us death before nightfall.

Second Song
I am amazed that more than half a century
Has sloshed through the scuppers and that
No one has taken the time or the interest
To put down, for the children and for
Those that will come after them how it was
Out there where nothing breaks the wind's thrust,
Nothing interrupts dawn light or starlight
For day after night after day after night
While the coffee is made for each watch
And while food is cooked and served and
Sextants are sighted and lifeboats checked
And men go to sleep so close to each other
That one's breath becomes the breath of another
And where one learns to lock dread away
Having no control at all over one's living or dying.
It is those arms and backs, that energy that moved
Those cargoes whose makeup in the holds and
Up on deck became the engines of war. Those B-25s
Lashed down without wings were lifted over the side
By the cables stretched between booms as
The ship anchored out off the beach at
The Russell Islands, north of Guadalcanal,
While the palm trees swayed in the eyes
Of the plow jockeys from Missouri who had
Grown up the Week before when the first Zeros
Had strafed the convoy the first time.
      Yes, the Admirals had their responsibilities
And yes, they would tell, later
Much later, how they had sweated
As the enemy came tearing down the "slot"
In the heat of the night.
      There's more
Than one kind of sweat we learned—the sweat
Made by work in the heat and the one
Made by fear—and while sweating both
Kinds, off loading the planes and the gear,

(continued)

Wondering whether the skipper's aware
How salt those sweats are, out on deck,
In the tropics, at night I could not
But think how it always has been different
For those on the bridge and for
The rest of us down where we were.

Sixteenth Song

      So long ago and yesterday
Almost like the Ace of Spades
And the Jack of Hearts, depending
On which one you pick up and
Which one you lay down—they
Can be short, they can be long
An eternity ago, alive today
And this morning's coffee no
Different than the one I drank
The other day.   Like an accordion
Played by the hands of fate—
Time's tune can make you smile
And in the next instant cry. It can make you
Dream, and sigh, and make you remember things
Buried and gone so long ago.
It will draw a note out for so
Long a stretch you know it
Will never end and the days
And nights go by each with its own
Tempo and that boom can take
An hour to fall onto the deck
When it just misses you while
A week ashore can be gone
In only one hour's span— So
Long ago and yesterday all here
In the storeroom of the heart
That beats in time to keep
The rhythm of the accordion's tune
So that we can all end up dancing for a while,
Until it's time.

Jessica Lyn Elkins

JESSICA LYN ELKINS, born in Oklahoma, raised as a preacher's kid in Texas, moved to New Mexico in 1968 with her husband and two preschoolers. Earning a B.A. in Geography and Biology in 1976 from the University of New Mexico and a Master's of Arts in Liberal Education from St. John's College in 1988, she worked as a general contractor/builder and later as a human resources manager for multi-line auto dealers. Jessica grows herbs, watches birds, takes long walks, and writes from her North Valley home in Albuquerque.

DITCH WALK: HAIKU TRILOGY

I.

Brown fields of cut grass
Bundles of hay are waiting
To arrive at home.

II.

To running water
The leaves are falling golden
Into their last life.

III.

Listening for quiet
I hear the meadow lark's song
Can I hear between?

FIELD MORNING: HAIKU TRILOGY II

I.

Frozen dew glistens.
Lone coyote lurks by ditch
Wary of my scent.

II.

Silhouettes of geese
Feeding with lone sentinel
Ignore my slow steps.

III.

Cottonwoods rustle.
Shadows meet light on mud road.
Can I sense fall's death?

MORNING MEETING WITH COYOTE

I saw you again this morning.
Startled from the brush
You ran down the road ahead
Tan coat shining, four paws softly hitting hardened ruts.

Your instincts took you to the center
The middle of the field where you felt safe.
Stopping to see if I was a threat,
Ambling quickly to the ditch,
Disappearing into the eastern light pouring over dry weeds.

You saw me again on the other side.
Standing alert, head cocked
Waiting to see if I would pass.
You circled back, patient tolerance of your interrupted hunt.

Will we meet again?

COYOTE ON THE PLAZA

Glancing through the upstairs window
Movement catches my eye.
Opening the balcony door
I stand in the bright sunlight looking down on the red plaza.

Yes, it is coyote
Ambling through the plaza, staying on the edges.
Unaware of my gaze,
Nosing up to the half opened garage door.
Stops, looks, and slides from view.

Were you really there?
The instant passed so quickly.
Who should I tell?
You faded away before my eyes.
Why did you come?
You were unafraid, only curious to see where I live.

ONE HUNDRED AND ONE CRANES

November late afternoon, clear, chill.
The sounds resonant from above, calling, calling.
V-shaped patterns circling, dissolving and merging
High, so high the eyes must squint to see.

In the blue, surrounded by abstract forms of clouds
Stark forms and black tipped wings, necks outstretched
Calling, calling to each in the group, south, south
Fly on to rest and food.

Why did I count, why was it so important?
The numbers change at our whim,
Forgotten, then remembered,
Hunted, then protected.
One hundred and one, I wish you speed to safety.
Winter home.

A KESTREL IN A COTTONWOOD TREE

Thoughts on Politics, December 19, 1998
Impeachment of a President

Bird perched high, scanning carefully.
Gnarled tree, rooted tenaciously.
Blue sky, glowing splendidly.

Bird unaware of world events.
Tree growth spanning generations.
Sky endless and unlimited.

Woman, take these signs and wonder.
Indifference of nature never changing.
Humanity's dreary problems, how transient.

YEAR PAST AND PRESENT

Last year old friends departed.
Disturbed.
A Brief interruption.
Buried.
Last year new friends appeared.
Welcomed.
A new accommodation.
Begun.

Last year family crisis summoned.
Saddened.
New thought of death.
Wondered.
Last year love expanded.
Sustained.
A satisfying life.
Fulfilled.

This year new challenges beckon.
Exciting.
The unknown road ahead.
Seeking.
This year old fears spurned.
Healing.
A simple existence.
Hoping.

THE ROCK
For my friend

Shaped by wind, water, fire, and earth's stress
Tumbled, cracked, roughed, broken away, smoothed.
The rock found a resting place
Only to be discovered anew.

Our self is the rock.
Our inner, hidden self that abuse, distress, conflicts reveal.
The finely grained beauty, the true self like the rock
Revealed and exfoliated by life.

Wash water over the rock.
Pour Spirit over self.
See the true rock/self.
A tempered object of beauty,
Found and treasured by friend and God.

Doris Fields

Doris Fields is a writer and visual artist. She conducts creative and technical writing workshops throughout New Mexico, has read her poetry in the U.S. and in the Caribbean, is a recent inductee into Live Poets' Society, an eclectic collection of northern New Mexico poets, and just completed her second manuscript of poetry. Doris has taught a course, *Her Own Voice: Black Women Writers,* for the past twelve years and is currently pursuing a Ph.D. in Intercultural Communication at the University of New Mexico. Doris is a founding mother of *Us 'N R Art: Women Artists of African Descent,* an art exhibition held in Albuquerque annually, and recently held an exhibit of her art in a Santa Fe Canyon Road gallery. She is also a veteran 20-year public health worker with the New Mexico Department of Health.

I AM FEARFUL
(take me to sea)

to speculate the ocean's pull to me
must always
return quickly to conscious
lest I learn
to walk on water
drink dry the sea
smile at the internal pound
of my lungs bursting
join my cousins
aunts uncles
grandmothers grandfathers
friends
on the path back to mother

black as night is my face
heart black, too
soul, indeed
my marrow is black

night is the mother father
sister lover who embraces me
licks my face clean in the mornings
nourished by my salt
sea water she calls it
mesmerizing sea water
says it calls her, too
says she can't help herself
does not want to
has no desire to

I want to cling to the ocean water
like star fish to mussels
at the base of boulders

(continued)

I want to go with every grain of sand
towed in the under current
to the deepest parts of the ocean
then I want to climb the hill
out of the sea to home

I fear to speculate the ocean's
pull to me
sometimes I am up to my nose
in the sea
before I catch myself
following the black
then the gray
then the white grains of sand
know some of it
is millions of Africans' bones
pounded by deep waves
into the finest softest, powdery sand

I like what it feels like on my skin
between my toes
the sand is my mother father sister cousin
aunt uncle
powdered to perfection
pulling me to the sea
shifting sand deepens my thought

I have made friends
with sand dollars
blue crabs and shell homes

still
I fear
to speculate the ocean's pull to me

10–16–97
octoba

EL HIJO DE LA LLORONA

today she will look for faces
find spirits of the sea
is it a face if it has only one eye?
it is a face   sand dollars and rocks
lie down together in high tide

the heart is a rock   has a face on one side
big heart   big face   big spirit

I want to see what the sea   brings me
el nino negrito tal vez es el hijo de La Llorona
buscando la madre   la mama de los hijitos
cerca del agua

what the sea brought   no drought   no doubt
empty shells and Africans' bones

a heart strong enough to survive
the tide   intact   in fact chambers
pumping searching for a body   any body
strong enough to beat   time like that
deserves a good heart

El Nino   is a BAD monahema
teeth   eaten out by time   and plankton
homes for small soft crabs
side walking   non-talking   teeth
kidney condensed to a stone itself
waiting for the right moment

see the sea   belching sand dollars
that mount volcanic rocks with eyes
eyes searching for the souls of Blackfolks
eye balls   rest on rocks   bore eye holes
for sea urchins to see their predators

(continued)

black skin beaches bear holes for
the baby boy   yo quiero saber que va a pasar
cuando el niño haya terminado
where will the ocean's edge rest
will the beaches go out to sea
the current beach return a desert
will 50 miles ocean lake desert return to Peru
will the beaches in the bay
yield green flowers and blue

does the ocean ever plan to return the children
or the ancestors
will it ever belch up every unresting
bone and body
sacred sacrifices to the gods

when will the ocean know enough is enough
will el nino be enough
will la nina have to belch herself out from
the sea grave   will the entire path of souls
bones from this coast to Africa's west
have to rise in cane
cease to be waves and sand grains
connect every heart   liver   bigger whale
become whole and march right out of that sea
before the ocean gets it
how loud does La Llorona have to scream
before the sea lets them go home
just how fiercely will every heart have to beat
before peace comes
the calamity is not that they are lurching
but that they are not respected   not understood
still strong enough to show the world their souls
¿que cree que paso con La Llorona?
¿y que tiene para ella?

3–6–98
machi

THE CHILDREN LOSE

children
o child
strong baby of Afghanistan
minus one land mined leg

o child of Treblinka
the light twinkles without your glasses
without your mother who has gone to the gasses

sweet child of Sarajevo
your city is so beautiful
but you must climb the canyon and leave it

na wewe habaari
black daughter of Soweto
with tight woolen hair
and diamonds for eyes

brown girl from Managua
la quien habla solamente el español
la quien quiere solamente vivir

chiquita de San Salvador
con chinitos negritos
pale child of Appalachia
veins growing through translucent temples

o child of Detroit's rubber sidewalks
and steel bullets   one eye gone and your mother dead

o wasted child of the street
sweeper

sweet children of innocence
bold eyes of pain
gut torn by hunger
or bullets or both

(continued)

scars on the vein
lesions on the brain

bury the white shroud   beside your mother

bury the white soldier
beside the back of your burning nostril
follow the tracks
back to sweet home
and love and warmth

run as fast as you can
make a set of concentric circles
around your target
and feed the marrow
that is your upbringing

sweet child of Sarajevo
sweet child of Soweto

sew your toes back on
walk the ten miles to your mother
dusting gold off the diamond back haven

hijita de Managua
grace the red fire
of the evening sky
with your burning lips
and kiss away the pain

misplaced geeche of Appalachia
play a sonata on your banjo
to call all the hogs in

(continued)

Pakistani migrant of Mujahideen birth
hold up the bloody sheep
pile one more brown rock in the hole
plant potatoes and wheat
in the mine fields

Pilgrim
up south in the promised land
remove the wheel you invented
take advantage
of the golden black wax
walk on water across the continent

disrupted feature de la bamba
spin a rocket to the moon
turn back the hands of time
be the first to land

o child of the weeeak
and week
and weak
bury the white rock
in an unmarked grave
he has no kin
and the anthropologists
will dig the challenge

o child of the world
o 99%
know yourself
know each other

o child of Sarajevo
o child of San Salvador
        of West Bank
        of Afghanistan
        of Ireland
        of Tibet
                (continued)

                    of Detroit
                    of Gaza
                    of Dachau
                    of Sudan
                    of the Zulus
                    of Bergen-Belsen
                    of Auschwitz
                    of the Hutus
                    of Treblinka
          o black child of Soweto
          ulifanya niini
          absorbing all light
          you are homeless
          or you are dead
          tonight

                              8–19–87
                              agosto

Henry C. Finney

HENRY C. FINNEY is a professional artist and writer and was a former sociologist for many years at the University of Vermont. He turned to full-time writing and painting in 1994, the year he completed his MFA in painting and printmaking at Pratt Institute in New York. He studied at the Vermont Studio Center, where the influence of Vermont painter James Gahagan—a student and colleague of Abstract Expressionist artist Hans Hofmann—was especially formative. Finney has a Ph.D. in sociology from the University of California at Berkeley and a B.A. in anthropology from the University of Michigan. In recent years he has taught art at the University of Vermont and the Massachusetts Institute of Technology. His recent published essays and invited lectures deal with art criticism, Zen Buddhism (of which he is a practitioner), and the social organization of the contemporary art world. He is also a poet. His art has been widely exhibited in Vermont and the Northeast, including New York City, and he is part of numerous private collections, including IBM's. He is one of the artists in the 1995 Marquis' *Who's Who in the East* and the 1998 *Who's Who in the West*. Until recently he was represented locally by Santa Fe Contemporary Art. He has curated several local contemporary exhibitions, including, most recently, "Contemporary Art 1998," with Stuart Ashman, Director of the Museum of Fine Arts in Santa Fe, as juror. In early 1998 he spent two months as a juried artist at the Dorland Mountain Arts Colony in California as both poet and painter. In 1998 he had a solo exhibition in the new quarters of the Art Center at Fuller Lodge in Los Alamos, New Mexico, where he now lives and works.

CIRCUS

Awakening, I see the shades of others stir.
I see what isn't there.
You are not there, nor I.
The leaves rustle to mark time.

Put aside what you know;
               don't select what is beautiful.
Just see what is there,
               visible only in your
               peripheral vision,
                    a blur that dissolves
                    when you look directly.

Slow down.

You must stop thinking to see
               the creatures who
               fade at dawn.
If you rush, they retreat
               like frightened fawns.

Study the bark of a Ponderosa,
               vanilla microcosm of an
                    endless vertical world,
               ragged black cracks of time
                    splitting the years of rosy tan.

Who lives here?
Rushing off to the next intention,
               the next plan,
                    the next hope,
                        the next ambition,
You will miss the circus that is in town,
               playing just for you.

FOUNDATION

Safe, secure, heels printing
        dry rings in hard sand,
I wander through tongues of foam
        left by thundering breakers;
Endlessly they roll in,
        soft roar filling the haze.

But churning cascades mesmerize,
        crash after merging crash.
I am drawn in; my will dissolves.

Foam swirls past...
        foundation washes away...
                stones loosen under my feet...

Suddenly, unawares,
A bone-jarring thump
        into the clattering gravel,
And a vigorous salty swim.

OCEAN GAMES

We walk on the ocean sand for hours today,
        slowly, feeling the air,
        listening to the salt flume.

Thundering surf whitens the world,
        crash after crash merging
        until their progeny, energy spent,
        lap tongues of foam at our feet.

Children run after receding washes to plunge their
        sticks yet further in,
        scream as they race
                back to escape the next wave's assault.

I, alert to impending defeat,
        reading all the sea signs to predict my range,
Walk at the edge,
        knowing any misjudgment,
                will force my retreat.
With a thrill, I judge the entire sea,
        understanding it all for my intended victory,
        until,
                an unreckoned flood rushing on,
                        I give hasty ground.

Tiny birds, legs strumming invisibly, rush
        each ebb to feed in measured flurry,
then scurry back,
        droll unison flock,
                from the closing foamy attack.

An unexpected surge chases them into flight;
Unruffled, they return.

                        (continued)

Instinctively, we dance with the forces of our destruction.
                    We tease fate.
Through our games we merge, momentarily, with the sea,
                    with sand, foam, wind,
                    with white sound,

Until,

                    thunder fading,
                    the game ceaseless even in our absence,
We forsake the dissolving
                    border zone and return to roads we know.

SKI LODGE

Sun glares off brilliant snow,
        off a hill of tracks,
                too hot to view.
Scintillating yellow through the lids,
        my eyes glow with heat.

Undulating babble all around reveals
        ordinary ultimate absorption in fun;
Every run is a tunnel to the cosmos.

Figures carve by,
        too swift to measure,
        no beginning, no end.

They gather on the deck, in the sun,
        to report how a sprawling fall
        brought them back to existence,
And then, after hot chocolate, how they will transcend
        their bodies once again.

What could be more direct?

"The sodas are sixty-five cents, Mama."
Indeed they are, and what a bargain!
Each taste can send you to another world.

CYCLES

I awake during the day,
        sleep at night.
The transitions are difficult.

Still lost in dim mazes of sleep,
        stumbling upon bones of old friends,
Early dawn in this solitary place,
        is a time heavy with ghosts and demons.

Then, slowly enveloping the trees,
        sunlight returns.

During the day, I paint.
Some of my canvases glow and sing;
Others refuse their favors,
        remain mute.

Then again,
Late in the afternoon of this live-oak winter
        life drains away,
        leaving cotton mists,
        a faint glint from some distant vineyard.

Gradually, darkness rises like vapor from the earth.
My friend the owl comes to hoot.

During the night endless, unconscious, nameless,
I fend off madness with red coals,
        return to my origins,
        hear the stars sing.

It is our cycle, laughing and crying,
        exulting in the rediscovery of colors,
        grieving for lost times.
I forget even to ask who I am.

MOTHER AND CHILD

A child shrieks in the black of night.
She cries for us all.
Who now will hold the mother?

FAREWELL

At last,
After years of darkness
Everywhere I hear the rustle of cottonwood
            leaves fluttering in the sun;
And in their midst
My dead mother and father quietly converse.

Beverly Fox

BEVERLY FOX eloped at 17; widowed at 21 by the Viet Nam war. She grew up in the heady sixties in the race riots of Los Angeles and New York. While living in the Deep South she joined the NAACP. Experiencing the legal impotency of women through rape and sexual harassment she became an active, verbal proponent of NOW and ERA. Her efforts were validated by J.Edgar (Hoover) when placed on his "list," an honor she fondly embraces to this day.

After passing the torch of activism to a less jaded generation she moved to the deserts of the Southwest. She now lives in the quiet solitude of northern New Mexico. Free to proceed through life at her own pace, she finds herself falling into the rhythms of the ancient world around her.

Beverly understands the fragility of life and land through the experiences of her own biochemically poisoned body. She finds this interconnectedness to often be the focus of her writing.

THE LEGACY

In the Dream Time streams ran full and free,
beasts held dominion and
stars shone brightly in the night sky.

The Ancients listened to their prehistoric desert.
They knew the delicacy of the land and the many
moods of nature.

We have forgotten lessons long-ago learned and
have evolved into a state of non-communion with
our world.

We need to once again listen
to remember the Dream Time.

A QUIET HOLIDAY

The ancestral mind holds a point of knowing
and yet not thinking—or even truly understanding.

In this place is the beginning, and end, of hope.
A place to visit every now and then, if only
to nod a casual hello to.
It holds a wisdom of its own; a wisdom as old as
humanity.

It's a good place...
a wonderful celebration of one.

GOD'S FACE

While growing up I had a "special spot" in my
hometown. A secluded area of spongy, green
grass, crowned with an ancient willow.

When I die, God, please allow me to sit under
that willow once again and watch the migrating
geese, in harmonious and purposeful agreement,
fly southward.
Could I watch another sunrise over the steamy
waters of Hudson Bay and see the aurora borealis
illuminate the Arctic night sky?
Or rest for just a moment, on the porch of a
small wooden cabin to watch a sleepy Nova
Scotian village tuck itself in for the night?
Might I watch the sun passionately kiss the
Sea of Cortez goodnight?
Could I feel the white sands of St. Simon's
warm my feet as a gentle breeze brushes
my cheek?
Would you give me a desert morning to hear a dove's
song or watch a hummingbird's flight?
Or stand barefooted in a cool mountain stream and
feel a trout brush my ankle in his way downstream?

When I die, will you allow me these treasured
moments so that I might hear your voice and
see your face for peaceful eternity.

MYSTICAL REGENERATION

Insects in pagan pitch dance in the moonlight
and make love beneath the grass.

An ocotillo standing tall and proud,
spreads its thorny fingers in hushed silence
as ancient hill-shadows advance.

Clouds sweep through the Southern sky,
the monsoonal sauna slowly lifting its
heavy hand in relief

Lazy thoughts and a leadened heart rejoice in
this undersong of creation;
a cosmic breeze slowly etch-a-sketching a heart clean.

UNKNOWN GENERATIONS

Parents, in hopes of raising them right, have
made this town their home. Tall gingerbreads,
a century old, house their dreams of
red, white and blue, edged in gold.
Apple orchards, skating ponds and self-grown
foods are nothing special, only and simply expected.
The children romp and play and eat beside
a picturesque creek. Up above, and down
a little, rolls on an old canal, spilling its
waters to a thousand crevices, making it their own.
While parents sleep soundly, little eyes peer
out, catching all—but understanding little.
Under the moonlight and around the bend
Shadowy monsters stealthily creep on.
They dump their canisters deep in the swamp
and watch as the ooze bubbles up to the top.
The insidious liquid settles where it always has.
Where all is black and silence deafens
and birds lie lifeless on the swamp.
"Come!" scream the children in daylight
playing. "Let's go into the creek to find more
circus frogs, or maybe a dead kitten."
As years go by with parents long in the
heavens, the children once more say
"Come, let's play." But now the creek has
stopped its chattering. There are no more
frogs, only dead kittens.
And where, they ask, are younger children to
live in the gingerbreads and have a life
worth living?
"Come, little children, and tell us now
Just why you won't e'er be born."

WIDOW'S WALTZ

She lies in her bed as a crumpled
leaf lies on a forest floor.
Without conscious thought she gazes
into the face of the moon with a wayward
glance at the nearby star.
Her body twitches with sudden shock
and then relaxes, lest she forgets her pain.
She is as much earth as she is heaven
and both beckon with a siren's wail.
Her muscles unfold and peace is found
as she understands that all must be
left undone when time to go.
Life, by its nature, will be continued
by those she's touched; she must bid farewell.
She shifts slowly in her bed and feels
her husband's smile as his hand
caresses her withered brow.
Gently she drifts to her timeless sleep
and dreams of buttercups and waltzes
in the moonlight glow.

Halsted

HALSTED

Painter/Poet
A woman whose life was changed
By fate
Thinking it a disaster
She found a miracle.

IRON

I used to love to iron
baby clothes
shirts
dinner napkins
but that was when flat was still flat
round was round
a curve in the path was not an obstacle
but now I know
flat is not flat
and round not round
man can fall off the edge of the earth
and live with demons forever.
long, short, oval and square
none of them are what they were
in this adult world life is difficult
the nuance only that.
A child's world is cleaner
    neater
ironed
unless he is starving
    even that can be tidied up.

dec 7th 1996
pearl harbor day

DREAM CATCHER

dream catcher
made by an Amazon woman
hung on the Russian clock
from the nuclear submarine
bought from a catalogue

dream catcher
dreams spill through like mercury
staining my very breath
tainting me awake or asleep
I see what I do not wish to see
Instead do your job
catch the dreams so no fear will befall me
becalm me
in the Arctic jet stream
let me be

I look out for another
But, no you   wrap me in images
colors, conditions
bind my hands with masking tape
I bellow
"I am not Christ"
the visions continue
forcing me up at five a.m.
          to write
another story of another dream
you did not catch for me

Dream catcher,
feather and bead
circle of bent wood
feather and blue bead
                              string net
how could you catch me so   relentlessly.

Feb 1998

I BUY

I buy the teeth of a dead woman
I buy the wing of an unknown bird
I buy a slave anklet in Turkey
800 silver, old,
I bet she danced for kings.
I buy the gold headed cane of Custer,
flocked skirts,
fur trimmed sweaters,
a tea set from the 1800's
a picture of trees bending over a thin road,
a road where cars can not travel.
I buy sandalwood incense, tarot cards,
horoscopes for me and my loved ones.
I buy cakes with sweet flowers on them
I buy milk to wash the sugar down
I buy playhouses and trees and install them
    in a non-existent setting
with sunsets
I buy music, CD ROMS, cable television,
clocks that no longer tell time
magazines, newspapers,
a first edition William Blake
I buy stocks to go up and bonds to go down.
I buy six piglets and a distressed wood sty,
dogfood, catfood, birdfood
indoor and out.
I buy until my money is gone and then I buy more.
I buy as if there were no tomorrow.

1999

CUTWORMS

cutworms
on the leaves
of my
hibiscus trees
make a lacelike work.
not embroidery by
hands of old women
keeping a craft alive,
not symmetrical,
not bobbins and spools.

I look closely, see myriads of small green caterpillars
with large black mouths
eating, eating eating
through the green leaves
soiling the nibbled
                    spots
then on to the others.

life in its complexity
has no love for these thin green things
called leaves
they are only food
perfect or imperfect, it does not matter.
sheep chew the grass,
monkeys turn back the browning skin of the banana,
the cutworms
lull the leaves into lace,
and we humans, no matter what we think
have our own unvalued place.

August 31 1998

NEW YEAR IS COMING

Someone is blowing up dried leaves
out there.
It is sixty degrees out there.
In November, there has been a gush of sixty degree days.
My mother is in an assisted living home.
My sister is getting her lips filled with collagen today.
I will join her at the Doctors and perhaps we will do lunch.
I am a recovering alcoholic.
Everyone in my family is recovering from something.
Of course one could extend this to the world not
just my family.
Sub-Sahara Africa is on my mind a lot.
The blacks down there, our species too, are dying
much too fast.
In five years their life span has shrunk by ten.
In the year two thousand men and woman are spending seventy
thousand dollars for a New Years' flaunt.
Stay in your bed it is much cheaper.
Stay in your bed today and no one will notice.
No one will notice if you take a cold glass of scotch
ice cubes, floating and tinkling.
No one will see,
they are too busy shopping for just the wrong Christmas present,
all anyone wants is money
or gold,
but that is a commodity and much too common
perhaps a many carat diamond.
Everlasting life is a good gift too.
Jesus was born in a manger two thousand years ago so man
could have everlasting life in the kingdom of heaven.
Why does no one act as if he believes it?

1998

APRICOT

She gave me an apricot this morning
                    creeping down the steps in the mist
Stumbling a little
It was six A.M.
she has gotten up earlier
                    to dislodge it from a tree
soul to soul
encryptions of sense and imagination
written on the apricot
a gift.

Bodies are vessels, bags
containing blood, bone, brain cells, capillaries
water and proteins.
moss coated dermas.

Oh, but the soul is a rogue agent
moving in and out at wish
you gave of yourself
your dreams, fears, mournings
                    rumblings of doubt
carved on an apricot

Thank you for your present.

August 1998

ICE BOATS

what is the matter
is it a dry spot
where divining for water is useless
ice, forty feet thick

I've seen ice boats, white moths, gliding
across thick ice
flying, fleeing the wind
eighty miles an hour
beautiful and fantastic
tacking with a single sail
right angles
one man in a helmet
turns down to the ice,
close as a speeding kiss
I have been promised a ride on an ice boat next year.
This year the season is almost over, sun streaks
weaken the ice.
The day, almost finished, the sun still glowing robust
resplendent setting skies calling the wild birds back north
the lips of spring are opening
time for the boats to bed down
on the straw where the rabbit spawn.

March 1999

DIAGONAL POSSUM

They are coming today
to check me out
do a mental assessment,
check mood, affect
congruence of emotion and thought
ask me to explain a proverb,
to count backwards
"Do you hear voices,
see things that others can not see."
Of course,
but I am smarter than that,
I once wrote the script
for mental assessments in a life
as remote as Moses,
as ancient as bulrushes
I parted the red sea for the schizophrenic
and made notations on commitments
when they had a working mental health policy
but now
I will smile, say I am fine,
am up in the mountains for solitude so I can write
play a diagonal variation of possum
then go back to firming out the memories
just in case
this time
I understand what happened

1999

Honorable Wyatt H. Heard

THE HONORABLE WYATT H. HEARD was a State District Judge for twenty-one years, retiring in 1991. Since then he has been doing mediations and arbitration in Albuquerque, New Mexico.

ST. FRANCIS

I am a guest of him whose house is swaddled in gardens,
A day of leisure,
With no obligations, away from home,
Where not even family or house or neglected ground
Can lay claim to attention.

As I gaze down on the green foliage
And feel the warm sunshine on the back of my neck,
Attention is drawn to a small ceramic statue—
St. Francis—holding a bowl of water in one hand
And a bird in the other.

By some criteria, it could be said St. Francis was insane:
        He turned his back on his Family fortune
        He proclaimed for himself, salvation would come when
            He identified with the poor,
        He accepted what God said to him: "Rebuild my
            Church."
If any of our children came to us
And recited the declarations above,
Would not society agree with us if we said: "Are you crazy?"
        Turn the other cheek,
        Forgive and love your enemies,
        If you have two coats, give the other to the poor,
        The meek shall inherit the earth.

The world—these statements at best are silly.
Yet eight centuries later, we still make small statues of
St. Francis and place them in our gardens.

On some deeper level probably not visible we are saying:
        St. Francis got it right; we belong to God
        Only by belonging to others.

JACK

There he stood with a
Glint in his eye,
The smile crept into the corners of his mouth,
He would shuffle away like a boxer would do,
But you knew the holy spirit
Had just made a visit.
The care he had for you was
Human but you knew
It transcended that level,
When we see and feel
it we know this is
The real article but
Description defies our vocal cords.
He would say "Hi," one
word, and then ten thousand words
Flooded around you.
The Lower you were on
The social pecking order
His touch was like Jesus' when he embraced
The leper.
We want our good deeds
somehow recorded
But not him
He bobbed and weaved
His way through the
crowd;
But each one felt his
presence in some eternal sense.
How do we distill
The essence of this man?
Maybe as one of the apostles was described,
"There is Nathaniel in whom
there is no guile."

SEVENTY

After seven decades
Once again ushered into
Campus life
Where the trumpet of
trade begins to be dimmed.
The sound of art intrudes
into the crossroads of civilization
and stands against
the ravages of time
proclaiming the fearless
truth.

Truth words do not
Perish but on waves
Of sound fly abroad.
Why is it in youth
we are so sure about life,
only to awake in
the late decades
hearing the vibrations
of ambiguity which threaten
us in youth.

But in elder age uncertainty
Feels like
Comfortable old shoes.
Maybe it is as
one sage declared,
"Certainty is the sin
of bigots, terrorists, and pharisees."
Compassion make me
think I may be wrong....

DADDY

There he sat on the lawn furniture:
with his small portable
radio tuned in on the
baseball game.
The voices of my children
and others filled the air.
He was not the focus of
their attention but
they knew he was there.
Waiting as a patient
mentor if needed.
His massive frame and
those huge hands which
in former days used a
rope and an ax,
now simply turned the
dial on his radio.
Three decades ago my
judgment was flawed of him
that is now in the past
never to be retrieved.
Hopefully it will give me
pause when my judgment
of someone else is not
tempered with mercy.
These lessons extract a
toll on us, but maybe,
just maybe compassion
will not only be allowed to
surface but flood all our
cells and we are becoming
something new

BIRTH

Out of the womb of God
we left the garden for good
a flaming sword symbolized,
we would never return.
It was ordained to be
that by that birth our cloak
of innocence was shed.

Later, God submitted
to be born by his own creation.
out of the root of Jesse,
as promised Abraham,
a hick Jewish girl
on the edge of an empire
was chosen as the vessel of deliverance.
Was God choosing submission
in the form of a babe,
so God could bring to pass,
a relationship with
his creation as a peer?

Maybe the mysteries of God
are to remain just that
a mystery.
The miracle of birth is
still beyond us even
as we reach for answers
To the universe.
Maybe Rilke perceived it,
"Living and embracing the
question is more important
than the answer."

CHANGE II

There we stand in confusion
In one hand touching the leaf moving
in our masculine wind,
In the other hand grasping the totem pole
buried deep in our feminine earth;
As if stretching to maintain the balancing
act, we connect the light and
darkness of our soul,
Maybe there is in this tension, sanity
in the midst of madness.

If we become lightning rods,
We change the electric energy of the
thunderstorm
As it runs into the earth
But it will not prevent the process of
the next storm from forming,
Chaos cannot be eliminated from
existence,
Nor can we cover over the calmness
which resides at the center of the
hurricane,
To deny the reality of co-existence of
chaos and order,
Is like creating a home of the living dead.
In our feeble attempts to anchor ourselves
in some concrete foundations of
our psyche,
Doesn't this say we can never choose
between chaos and order?
Hopefully we can live at the shifting
boundary between the two.

SACRED TRUST

Running against the tide;
Operating a feminist bookstore
For fifteen years:
This haven for women
Who have been locked out,
Wounded by a world which
Has failed to hear
The silence of rejection.

"Full Circle," a sacred trust,
If you please;
An island in the rushing
Rivers of this world.

The bottom line of the balance sheet
Was never an issue.
Its survival was paramount
In the hearts of
Anne and Mary.
It is time to pass it on
To the next torch bearers.

A symbol for the transition,
A red tail hawk lodged
Under the back stairs.
Found by them in shock
And dying of starvation.
Taken to a shelter
But too late for survival.

Perhaps a new cause or symbol,
Born for those who are beyond
Silence from the clatter of this world.

DO NOT BE AFRAID

There I sat on Maundy Thursday
as they stripped the altar,
the disciples riding the
crest of the wave with
this gifted Rabbi,
also must have felt stripped.
They pierced his side
and the gloom descended like a fog,
which could only be severed with a sword,
and their Kingdom
appeared to dwindle
before their eyes,
and fear lay hold of them;
Not only was their power
vanquished but
terror struck and
their survival was in fact at issue.
As one sage said,
"The game of life is not so much in holding
a good hand, but in
playing a poor hand well."[1]
In the deepest forest of Canada
one Shaman was asked,
"What was God like?"
"He speaks like the storm and the wind,
but at times his
voice is feminine and like a child."
"What does God say?"
"He says do not be afraid."[2]

---

[1] H.T. Leslie
[2] Carl Lumholz, Norwegian Anthropologist

Gerry Hotchkiss

GERRY HOTCHKISS was in magazine publishing for forty years in New York, Chicago, Boston, and London, UK. He worked for *Life, Newsweek,* and *Look* and was publisher of *Psychology Today, Science Digest* and *50 Plus,* which was renamed *New Choices.* He and his wife of forty plus years live in Tesuque, New Mexico.

IS EVER THERE MORE MISCHIEF
THAN IN A WOMAN'S BEAUTY

Is ever there more mischief
Than in a woman's beauty.
From childhood, all compliments
And fancies dim her senses.

She sulks
And casts a dull eye, lest
Her looks confuse the issues
Of your mind.

But be she insecure,
A moment's twinge, unsure,
She plays upon her charms
As swiftly as the morning glory
Opens at first light.
Her eyes bedazzle,
She gains her point
And looks away.

Take notice of her costume,
Style, any outer complement.
Wary be of flattery;
She'll bore of your intent.

Shut from your face her eyes,
Address the earnest voice,
She'll perk up, smirk, sit up,
Take note, rejoice.

(continued)

Be not deceived,
Her beauty's well received,
Acknowledged,
She knows it is her prize
Too quickly won.
Reward her for her strive
At talents less overt,
Engage her mind.

Joust with her intellect
Though she suspect it is
A tilt at other things
She'll play the part.

When her voice drops low,
A whisper, sibilant,
As soft as milkweed,
Swift to escape your ears
Or eyes, as she intends,
Look straight at her.

Right through the iris,
Smile.
Her beguile rewarded
She'll laugh
And like the feline creature
That she is, ignore you,
Retreat a distance
And begin again.

RUSSIAN OLIVES

Pinon and juniper dot the hill,
Chamisa outline the valley,
Blue penstemon and wild aster
Nestle between yellow sunflowers
While on the mountain we await the golden aspen.

Yet all around
In earth bone dry or soaking wet
Russian olives sprout
And grow as fast as jackrabbits,
While we watch the billowed clouds on the horizon.

Planting itself;
Growing so quickly unattended,
Unneeding of our attention,
Independent, self-sufficient
While we worry over brighter flora.

Its limbs,
Heavy with yellow-green seeds,
Hide finches and robins,
Mountain bluebirds and a flicker,
While we refill the hummingbird feeder.

Windy afternoons
Break ponderosa pine,
Chase ravens into their nests
And cloudbursts scuttle coyotes
While slender, reedy Russian olives, carefree, wave.

We want the grand.
The roadside showy colors,
Majestic mountains quaking,
Sunsets exploding, the Milky Way,
While all around us the quiet olive beauty stands.

INFINITY

A grammar school boy,
With tousled hair
Going nowhere,
Sitting in a barber's chair

Looking in a mirror.
To his front and back
A mangled sack
Of unruly black.

A jar with shaving brush,
Brown razor strop,
And reflected on top
His face, his hair a mop.
The smell of lavender,
Between the snips
And scissors clips,
Permeated his skin, his lips.

He closed his eyes,
Daydreamed, wandered
Afar, a great void beyond
His perception; he pondered
That new idea at school.
To understand he could not pretend,
Drawn with a connecting bend,
No beginning, no end.

His head in the mirrors,
Smaller, smaller he counted
Receding images, encountered
Infinity. "No end," he shouted.

The barber through the mirror
Peered at him.
"I make it thin,
"What you mean, 'no end'?"

DRY WALLS

To shaggy turfs
And peeling birches
Dry walls call.
Each stone placed
In consonance.

Strict rhythm
Dances Queen Anne's lace
With elder maples bending the hill.
Hard orders
In a lime and acid soil.

A backache
Worked to plant these boulders.
It was not easy to collect
Such angular New Englanders
In unison.

My father's tenor
Refused earth's uneven tempos;
Cold notes of hoarfrost
Left unmelted.
He was uneasy.

Stem measures
Concealed romantic songs.
No mortar allowed, no convenience
Forgave his final beats
Exactly placed.

Too late a stone, upturned,
Dislodged a bird's nest.
"Sing to me now," a sparrow calls
"Dry walls, dry walls."

Bonnie Lupien

BONNIE LUPIEN has been writing poetry since 1973. She feels it's a wonderful way to express her feelings. She is a member of the Live Poets' Society and started a poetry group in Durango, Colorado, called Poets of the Heart. Bonnie also has a passion for dancing and teaches Country Western dancing. Expressing the rhythm she feels in her soul, she is also into drumming and singing.

She is enjoying being a Lay Minister with Unity in Spirit in Durango and connecting with friends. She also is the Moderator for a spouses' forum in the Young Presidents Organization of Los Angeles. She enjoys flying and was a private pilot.

She really loves hosting parties on her Shalako Ranch with her husband, Bill. They have been married 36 years and have a daughter, Susan.

CANDLE FLAME

My heart expresses an endless stream
    Of love it wants to pour out to others;
It goes out to young and old,
    Fathers and mothers, sisters and brothers.

It flows out to the poor and the rich,
    It doesn't seem to matter to me;
Even to strangers I meet on the street,
    It feels good when a smile I see.

I need to connect and share myself,
    Let them know they have a friend;
Someone who sincerely does care,
    Being with them is time I'll spend.

To give them encouragement and support,
    To give them feedback that I've heard;
To give them advice if they ask,
    Feels right, and I'll keep my word.

There are times I need alone
    To become reflective and just be;
Who am I and what am I being?
    Is there something I should see?

After experiencing an inner silence,
    And listening for guidance which I need;
I'm ready to go back into the world,
    To spread joy as a seed.

By giving out warmth, what do I get?
    A glow inside me I can't explain;
I'm like a candle whose flame lights up
    With radiance to shine, not contain.

SPIRIT

I am with you, whispering,
Do you hear me?
Your mind is busy with details,
Do you want me?

I am with you every moment,
Do you need me?
You are anxious and worried,
Do you feel me?

I am at your beck and call,
Do you notice me?
All you need do is turn within,
Can you touch me?

We can never be separated,
Can you believe this?
Go ahead and give me a call,
You'll be submerged in inner bliss.

I'M NOT READY TO SAY GOODBYE

Her frail body has cancer hiding
As she lies on a special bed;
She's weak and pale but smiles at me,
And can laugh at something I've said.

Memories float out of my mouth
Into the space in between us;
Remembering happy times that we've shared,
Giggles right now are a plus.

I see I have five minutes left
To convey to her how I feel;
To say how much she's meant to me,
This time concept doesn't seem real.

No one knows how much longer
In her body she'll be here;
One more week? One more month?
My last moments with her, I fear.

I'm so sorry I have to leave her,
But with pressing events I need to;
Her time left is precious, I know,
I consider my words, want to get through.

I bend down to give her a hug,
Being careful not to hurt her;
I whisper "I love you" in her ear
As tears fill my eyes, she's a blur.

"Please tell me I'll see you again"
I silently and pleadingly want to ask;
I smile warmly at her instead,
This experience is a difficult task.

(continued)

My guts want to cry out loud,
To scream "It's too soon for you to die!"
To pound my fist, stomp the floor,
I'm not ready to say goodbye.

I turn to take a tearful walk
Out the room to get my things;
I hear her voice call out "Goodbye!"
I run back as if I had wings.

I wave and say I'll come again,
My voice quivers as I cry;
I leave her for the very last time,
I'm not ready to say goodbye.

November 7, 1997

FROM THE HOLE IN MY HEART

I am fortunate to have the means,
To buy a dress, a couch, a car;
Or a pearl, an opal, a diamond,
A drum, a piano, or a guitar.

But there are things I cannot buy,
Not then, not now, not ever;
I cannot buy deep friendship,
It doesn't matter how rich or clever.

My Visa card does not buy
Love to fill the hole in my heart.
My soul longs for true connection
With loved ones near or apart.

All the money in the world
Can't buy what we need to survive,
The material things that we own,
Aren't enough to keep hearts alive.

I find that I am very hungry
For nourishment that is not food.
I need communication from the heart
That fills me no matter what my mood.

Most important I can give
To my family or a friend;
Is heart-felt, unconditional love,
To flow between us without end.

THE NAKED TRUTH

As I stand before you now,
You may wonder who I am.
At first you see the outer me,
Dressed in whatever mood I'm in.

But it's only the outside of me
That your judging eyes take in.
The face, the hair, clothes and body,
Even the color of my skin.

The outer look shows only a part
Of who is beneath what you see.
Who is she really? What does she love?
What feeds her soul—there's the key.

What causes her to have pain?
What brings her heart much delight?
How does she become fulfilled?
Can she relax or is she uptight?

Does she ponder her wistful dreams,
Or does she only see dreams at night?
When angry, does she try to bury it,
Or does she feel strong and ready to fight.

Is she a true lover of words
Or do words of love really melt her?
Does she often rant and rave,
Or is her voice soft like a purr?

When you take the time with her
To understand and know her history;
You'll see beyond the outer clothing,
And touch upon her hidden mystery.

Then and only then you'll see
The naked truth of her that's real;
Not what you guess she might be like,
But the naked truth of how she feels.

THE MAZE

I'm stumbling around in a maze,
High walls stand on each side;
I make my way down the path
Wishing that I had a guide.

As I try out another way,
I have questions of every kind;
Where are answers to these questions?
Can't stop the chattering in my mind.

What should I do? When should I do it?
Agitation stirs me inside;
It's then I need to take a breath,
Letting these racing thoughts subside.

The only way to get true answers
Is to become silent and still;
I ask for guidance through this maze,
Surrendering my desires and my will.

In that very sacred place,
I feel connection with the Divine;
The maze in my mind has disappeared,
The answers were there all the time.

Mike Sutin

Mike Sutin's recent poetry celebrates, often with wit and humor, the universal human condition in the context of examining the complex sociology of northern New Mexico. Most of his didactic poems are the product of multi-cultural appropriation presented through the voices of others. His style is predominantly formal, using an iambic line with a frequent use of internal and end rhyme. A work of art "should carry its justification in every line." Mike believes that, in the fullness of time, the personal or publishing history of the author is not noteworthy. The two poems included in this volume are offered as a contribution to New Mexico's *Cuarto Centenario*. Please note his use of synonyms.

THEY CUT MY RIGHT FOOT OFF

Why did they cut my right foot off,
an inch above the ankle?
about four hundred years have passed,
What can explain the anger?

My foot, it was at first affixed
upon a bronze statue,
and honored me for leading men
to a remote venue.

In fifteen hundred ninety eight,
we left Bartolomé,
and came to Nuevo Mejico
in search of a sea way.

We went to find an ocean pass
to trade with the Chinese.
Instead, we found a river trail
we could not track with ease.

Our mission was to pacify;
to Christianize the flock,
to survey coastline harbors, straits,
to dig silver from hard rock.

My image was in Español,
not far from famed San Juan.
We overstayed our welcome there,
the pueblo put upon.

Our settlers were at first mere guests,
we made our selves at home.
But you can just imagine why
the natives bid us roam.

(continued)

We shoved across to Gabriel
(he, also named a Saint).
In pretense, peace was called for;
our move was just a feint.

This place across the river was
called Yoongeh Oweengeh.
We also moved those people out.
They had no right to stay.

Before we headed to the north,
we stopped at Acoma;
chopped one foot off each warrior
atop the sharp mesa.

Why did I do that dastard deed?
I heard it from afar:
Those ungrateful conquered killed
my nephew Zaldivar.

Our history records the fact
refused to us was food
to which we clearly had a right;
why, they were downright rude.

We shot six people in the town
and hung two Jumanos,
when they refused us nourishment
out in the Manzanos.

We had gone out to punish them
for grudging us a pittance.
They held us not in high regard:
our starved inheritance.

(continued)

We had proclaimed this land was ours
in honor of the King;
far those who did not understand,
no freedom was to ring.

The pueblo leaders all took oaths
as vassals to the Crown.
To pledge allegiance became
the prelude to showdown.

To hold me as royal liege lord,
they vowed homage and fealty;
but what I really wanted was
the gold beneath their realty,

How do you talk to Indians?
Would it not be futile
to elucidate in Spanish
the law was really feudal?

Our final destination place
was down to Santa Fe,
so we could build a holy church
in thanks to God to pray.

And so, the quintessential symbol:
my hacked off appendage
is the most deserving icon
of this century's old age.

THE BALLAD OF BLOODY POPÉ

They tried to ban him from the Hall,
    the man they called Popé.
They said he was a deposed king,
    first of the red berets.

He led the Pueblos in revolt
    in year one-six-eight-o.
The villages were together,
    prepared for freedom's blow.

We properly proclaimed ourselves
    converts in faith and true,
and integrated ritual
    to please the you know who.

To sing, wear masks, and handle snakes,
    we were not heretics;
To dance and sprinkle sacred meal,
    nor were we lunatics.

But they called us "pagan"
    and "devil worshipper."
They tried to hinder how we prayed
    and danced with juniper.

The friars flogged our native priests
    and some of them were hung.
Our fetishes and plumes were burned
    and faith went underground.

(continued)

They killed us with their cholera,
        their measles and smallpox,
with whooping cough and epidemics,
        harsh schooled us in hard knocks.

Franciscan friars fought to earn
        our friendship and our favor.
The conflict led to cruel quarrels
        against the Governor.

At Mass, the civil leader cried
        "What you say, Priest, is a lie."
We did not know which one was right,
        and had no idea why.

The priests refused to let us dance,
        We wanted to bring rain.
They said our ancient Gods were bad
        and caused our hearts much pain.

Then many of us starved to death,
        our bodies left on roads.
No rain, no crops and disease left
        no one to haul their loads.

To unify was not our way,
        each village had its creed.
It was bad form to quit the norm
        and, so, no one would lead.

The straw that broke the camel's back
        five years before the break...
The soldiers seized our holy men.
        That was a big mistake.

(continued)

They reviled our men as sorcerers,
        charged with idolatry;
so who could hardly blame us
        for rejecting J.C.?

Whip lashed forty and strung up three,
        One was the fierce Popé.
Remembering the whipping post,
        He waited for his day.

To our local city San Juan
        he was a strong home boy.
He did not accept those lightly
        who would not shout "Destroy!"

The Pueblos rose on Lorenzo,
        the feast of August ten,
knotted yucca cords were untied.
        Four hundred said amen.

The missionaries martyred
        numbered twenty-one in all,
slain upon their holy altars,
        the new world's great down fall.

The chicanos raised two crosses
        on mounts in Santa Fe,
in tribute to three fathers
        who could not get away.

The remnant of the colonists
        were chased to El Paso,
then twelve years of freedom followed,
        thanks to the overthrow.

(continued)

Our tribes could not stay unified,
  found no success in blood.
La Conquistadora unleashed
  a brutal Spanish flood.

The survivors wrote down the words,
  and made this man a fiend.
The victors rewrote history
  and termed this chief unclean.

Perhaps it's true he promised that
  to kill a conqueror
will win a woman for a brave;
  but, this was outright war.

He rallied followers by lures:
  "If ten Spanish vanish,
then ten of our women are yours;
  And let us all feel mannish."

Your leaders all have blemishes
  from Jack and Ike to King.
Although they won their battles, they
  could not control their thing.

Take your president in D.C.
  He's nobody's fool.
To demonstrate democracy,
  Bill has to share his tool.

The noble Thomas Jefferson
  told you: "Refresh the tree,
from time to time with tyrant's blood
  to keep your liberty."

(continued)

"Each drop of blood drawn by the lash
        is matched by one from sword,"
the gentle Lincoln, he once said,
        "as a judgment of the Lord."

He strove to save a way of life.
        His motives, they were good,
and only by his enemies
        was he not understood.

Just like G. Washington,
        he has the right to stand
Inside the Nation's Statue Hall
        in honor to this land.

ENDNOTES:

1. "Popé Symbolizes Pueblo Revolt, Indian Survival," Mateo Romero, Pojoaque Pueblo Poeh Center, Op-Ed Page, *Albuquerque Journal*, July 19, 1997.

2. "Popé Doesn't Belong in Statuary Hall," Rubén Sálaz M., Historian, Op-Ed Page, *Albuquerque Journal*, July 30, 1997. "Popé symbolizes bigotry and hispanophobia more than Pueblo honor...Popé didn't have the character to lead pueblo society. He was deposed, perhaps executed, by the very people he led because he became a tyrant who demanded every conceivable benefit from his people."

3. *New Mexico*, Marc Simmons, The States and the Nation Series, pp. 63–76.

Arden Tice

ARDEN TICE taught Psychology at El Paso Community College from 1974 until 1981. She was a practicing psychotherapist from 1978 through 1988. Tice lived with Eskimos at Pt. Barrow, Alaska, and has traveled in Mexico, Greece, Spain, Costa Rica, and China. She has published four books of poetry including *Mi Casa es Su Casa* (1967), *Take It and Fake the Rest* (1974), *Wind in my Fist* (1990), *The Augmented Moon* (1991), and *A Naming of Women* (1994). *Looking for the Frontier* (Vergin Press, 1992) is a collection of her published essays and articles. She has presented her poetry at the University of California (Writers Week, 1986), Riverside Community College, and other universities, churches, clubs, etc. in New Mexico, California, and Texas. Today Tice volunteers in a writing workshop with veterans of the Vietnam War. Her collected works and papers are archived in the University of New Mexico's Center for Southwest Research.

Shards of memory, detritus from the great
upheaval: Ash and pumice though cold can be
used. We saw destruction, felt exhausted, but
bent and picked up bits and pieces and began to
build.

For the veterans in the writing
group who are building.

AN INTREPID ROMANTIC I SEARCHED

through all the pueblos of Mexico
looking for La Calle del Amor

I could not find that street although
I wandered up and down and all around

the vertical passages of Guanajuato   its
houses splashed with aqua blue and yellow too

seeking only a glimpse   a hint of when
where was that street   La Calle del Amor

in the ghostly El Santuario de Atotonilco
mottled by dust   pervaded pungency of pig shit

I saw the people flagellate themselves
with limp puny strands of purple hemp

were they searching for a pain   a thrill
that might still persist

even the drunken child with scarred lips failed me
thrusting his stump into my face for a cigarette

poor drunken monster child
I've known too many monsters to be moved

I

in the beginning

words in their teeth
heart in their hands
yellow leaves in the path

no hurry
one foot follows the other

II

in the beginning

they each had a sweet dream
the man tired of the long wait
the woman half awake.
with a quick glance goodbye
a staccato embrace under sun dappled pine
for a moment their eyes met straight
        did you listen to the music
        some he muttered
        they were   she said   a gift for your
            birthday
        she did not say   I wanted to give you
            everything
it was not necessary   he knew and she
        knew
there was nothing either could do
but turn hearts on their heels
memorize the lingering day

III

in the beginning

their other lives winding down
seduced them

                    (continued)

yet how could they not have known as
into the mountains they climbed and talked
a little or a lot
the sun was warm on the rocks bearing ancient
        signs
further they climbed
months like years passed
the autumn days held fast
beneath the pines
watching kindling catch fire
they lay in the cold
his fingers barely brushing the map of her road
there were no words in that quiet
power and hope rose
they had a secret they shared
which had been unbearable alone

IV

in the beginning

this emblazoned october breeze
can not bring ease
cascading maples can not relieve
the too long wait
vermillion leaves carouse
like a thousand firey tongues
        that play over and over the riff
        love destroyed   must be regained
        timewarped love into pain
        yes   I want your hands
                I want your lips
                'though every kiss a tear
                'though every touch a tease
                and every riff must end
how then can I admit untimely love
let its hungry arms enfold me
give it my ample breast
while I drift and fall with each red leaf

(continued)

while I fall and tumble into the abyss
while I dream and wait for the silence
after the riff

V
in the beginning

I was leaving
but you said wait
you must take this
you were right
knowing my hunger   you filled me
with pale green chili jelly
fed me on the end of your chopstick
pink shrimp
strings of vermicelli
my love   you fill my well

VI
in the beginning

the watermelon morning
grabbed my heart
stretched quiet hope
words if spoke
could not tell of
the void you crossed
giving yourself
waiting patiently for me
to admit my hunger
you are the first
you are the last

DESCENDING SEASON

we are all afraid of the night
when a shadow of light fades into blackness
we ache with emptiness
we want to be not alone

last night's full moon was rising
beyond the jagged line of charcoal

yesterday we walked   marveled at snowgeese
honking   V-splitting the pewter sky
downdrafted into winter river
these nine snow birds did in formation fly

                                             northwest

then wheeling round with updraft
they turned about joined the chevron cutting high
and twenty geese straight away did fly

                                          south
daybreak brings

                                          night lights
                                          nickel clouds
                                          black crows

their raunchy voices scavenge the

                                        concrete below
                                           (continued)

                                        vietnam's wall
is a glistening obsidian wave that begins small
rises to the day
carrying a spray of chiseled names

no storm wave could so implacable be
                                        our brains explode
                                                        implode
our eyes refract   the toy convertible
                                                the red rose

a squirrel on the grassy green passes a runner
who consults his watch

a time warped peace
while a man thrusts a quick handkerchief
into the back pocket of today's grief

slow slow we move along the wall
knowing there is no prize for us
knowing there is no prize for them

the frozen black wall that started small
now rises tall

but a stone wave cannot carry us
cannot lift our feet past sluggish day
once upon a tide in the affairs of time
we had a dream   o such a dream
I knew what it was to believe
do you know what it is to believe...before
the death of a dream

Pamela A. Wolff

PAM WOLFF is curious and purposeful. Like an investigative reporter, she is interested in people, the events affecting their lives, and the lessons to be learned from those experiences. Crossing borders and lines to meet others, she has traveled extensively in the U.S., Europe, and Mexico.

She admires Leonardo da Vinci, who expressed himself brilliantly as both artist and scientist. In her own life, she seeks and shares wisdom as a poet, an essayist, an engineer, and an activist. Although lacking Leonardo's talent, she adheres to his belief that knowledge comes from "knowing how to see."

Pam has considerable public speaking experience, has been a radio talkshow guest in Houston and Albuquerque, has written several articles that have been published in professional journals, and is a juried poet. She lives in Albuquerque, New Mexico, and shares her life with her two children, Alex and Elizabeth, and an over-grown Akita.

WHY PIRATES' DAUGHTERS SEE RED

Her blood
trickles to a fall
over the stainless edge,
his vain legacy
in her iron fist
staining the white-washed floor.

Splashing at her feet,
blood,
the silent sound between
her low-key life
and the landlocked folk
wary of fantastic tales.

Sword-swallowing women
have see-through lives,
know the pirate's sword
draws living color,
hope the Moving Finger
writes in vanishing ink.

Her eyes dilate as time
sweeps a nervous hand
over a sightless face
and shadows gouge plaster walls
like imprisoned thieves
slash colorless days.

She parts the red sea,
saving herself
one step at a time,
trailing footprints,
red footnotes,
to a hidden world.

IT TAKES A VILLAGE TO RAISE THE DEAD

She watched those public service ads
and wanted to believe
because they were made for women like her,
women with blind faith and black eyes,
crowned long ago by mothers
knitting black hoods for little girls;
swung by fathers stringing
fragile necks with man-made chains,
women with children and no family
bleeding from hands and feet;
willing to die for sins
if it really means
peace on earth,
goodwill towards men.

She was clueless about those ads
conjured by materialists,
mediums without a prayer
of helping women like her,
to keep women like her
up beat and on time,
keep them from disturbing
workplace sensibilities
offended by broken hands
struggling to keep up;
to keep children like hers
in line and on task,
keep them from burdening
schools too busy to dry tears
on chins of young students
struggling to keep up.

(continued)

So she jumps at her chance
keeping her eyes on heaven
keeping the faith
as witnesses
gaze upon
her leap of grace;
find shelter on sidewalks
beneath awnings
safe
from women like her
women with no where to go
but down
free
to fall
past gravediggers
whistling
in the dark.

RED HOT SLIDE

Scarlet streaks
  down beige skin
  drown in woman's pain
  seek the night's end
  pull the loose thread
  lives unravel
  beg for justice
  crushed by a gavel

I crossed the line
  I'm in no man's land
  there's no way out
  but down the red hot slide
  wet, hot, sticky slide
  found a free-fall ride
  on a midnight flight

Quick-silver dreams
  dance in woman's blood
  beating out a rhythm
  down the red hot slide
  wet, hot, sticky slide
  a moon cycle ride
  on a wild rip tide

Scar-lined skin
  like a weathered map
  shows where I've been
  not what I've seen
  rising to the surface
  of the red hot slide
  wet, hot, sticky slide
  took the freedom ride
  took a rose-sky flight.

HIGH PRIESTESS

Morning broke upon darkness
and shards of light
exploded
over jagged bones
protruding from a brittle land
abandoned by rain,
crazed by heat,
a burning white crucible
censing creosote,
rattling incantations
among silent scatters
of rock
harboring predator and prey,
stilled by radiance
spilling across the sky,
bleaching the atmosphere
until
heaven and earth vanished
and Eden
rose from the dead.

PROGENY

Summer's blue sun shadowed their fall;
followed their twisted flight,
fragile shapes lifted by
sweaty fingers of a trade wind
lining pockets of air
with leaves of tender green.

Light as color, they flicker-skip
in the shade of my arms,
glide past limbs that bore them;
tumble over roots seeking more
than the dry tongue of earth
is able to spit out.

Quenching thirst with dust, foundations
erode and barren trees
become brittle and break
under the weight of stone forests
leeching minerals for
monuments to their dead.

Dropping dead wood is not enough
to survive thrashing winds
and young leaves stripped away
before their time, before they're swept
from sight; into the folds
of a larcenist's coat.

WOMAN'S LAMENT

You know my presence

because I pass

in and out,

with flying colors,

your acid test,

with lightning speed,

your tainted offers,

beyond your sight,

close to the edge,

your fantasy.

C O L O P H O N

INTERIOR DESIGN/PRODUCTION

V. S. Elliott, SunFlower Designs of Santa Fe

COVER DESIGN/PRODUCTION

SunFlower Designs of Santa Fe

TYPEFACES

Minion (interior text) and University Roman (cover)

PRINTED AND BOUND IN THE UNITED STATES OF AMERICA

by De Harts Printing Services Corporation